LIVES
AND
TIMES

Martin Luther King Jr.

Peter and Connie Roop

Heinemann
LIBRARY

First published in Great Britain by Heinemann Library
Halley Court, Jordan Hill, Oxford OX2 8EJ,
a division of Reed Educational and Professional Publishing Ltd.

OXFORD FLORENCE PRAGUE MADRID ATHENS
MELBOURNE AUCKLAND KUALA LUMPUR SINGAPORE TOKYO
IBADAN NAIROBI KAMPALA JOHANNESBURG GABORONE
PORTSMOUTH NH (USA) CHICAGO MEXICO CITY SAO PAULO

Designed by Ken Vail Graphic Design, Cambridge
Illustrations by Sean Victory
Printed in Hong Kong / China

02
10 9 8 7 6 5 4

ISBN 0 431 02482 0

Some words are shown in bold, **like this**.
You can find out what they mean by looking
in the glossary. The glossary also helps you
say difficult words.

British Library Cataloguing in Publication Data

Roop, Peter and Connie
Martin Luther King - (Lives & times)
1. - Juvenile literature
2. - Biography - Juvenile literature
I. Title
362.4'1'092

This book is also available in hardback (ISBN 0 431 02483 9)

Acknowledgements
The Publishers would like to thank the following for permission to reproduce photographs:

Associated Press pp.18, 21; British Library p.22;
Corbis-Bettmann UPI pp.16, 17, 19; Martin, Phil p.20; Wide World p.23.

Cover photograph: Corbis-Bettmann UPI

Our thanks to Betty Root for her comments in the preparation of this book.

Every effort has been made to contact copyright holders of any material reproduced in this book.
Any omissions will be rectified in subsequent printings if notice is given to the Publisher.

Contents

The first part of this book tells you the story of
Martin Luther King Jr.
The second part tells you how we can find out
about his life.

Childhood

Martin Luther King Jr. was born on 15 January 1929 in Atlanta, USA. As a young boy he loved to play football, baseball, and the piano.

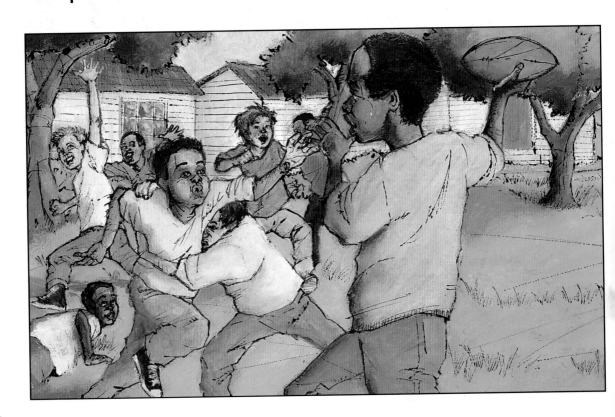

When Martin was young, there were **laws** that kept white and black people separate. One law said black children, like Martin, could not go to school with white children.

School

Martin wanted to change **laws** that treated black people unfairly. He worked hard and went to college when he was only 15 years old.

Martin wanted to be a **minister**. He went to study at a special school called a **seminary**. Here he learned about Mohandas Gandhi, the **nonviolent** leader.

Marriage

Martin met Coretta Scott when he was studying in Boston. In 1953, they were married. Coretta helped Martin with his work throughout his life.

In 1955, Martin received his **Doctorate degree**. He could now be called Dr King. That same year a black woman named Rosa Parks was arrested. She would not give up her bus seat to a white man.

Struggles

Dr King helped Mrs Parks. He organized a **boycott** of all the buses in the town of Montgomery. This made the bus companies lose money. The **law** was changed.

Some angry white people bombed Dr King's house. Dr King remembered Gandhi and said, "We must meet our white brother's hate with love".

Dreams

Dr King often broke **laws** that were unfair to black people. He was put in jail many times. Even when he was in jail, Dr King wrote books and letters to try to get the laws changed.

In 1963, Dr King gave a famous speech. He said, "I have a dream that little black boys and black girls will be able to join hands with little white boys and girls and walk together as brothers and sisters."

Death

On 4 April 1968, Dr King was shot and killed by someone who did not like the things he did. Americans everywhere **mourned** the death of this peace-loving leader.

Every year, in January, Americans celebrate Martin Luther King Jr. Day. They honour this **courageous** man who died fighting for **equal rights** for everyone.

Photographs

Dr King worked to change **laws** that kept black and white people separate. One law said that blacks and whites could not drink from the same water fountain.

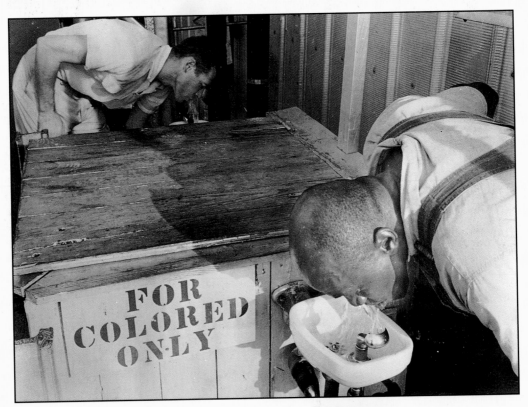

Martin Luther King was a popular
minister. Here he is speaking to the
members of a church.

Martin Luther King was famous after the Montgomery bus **boycott**. He gave speeches all over America asking for **equal rights** for everyone.

In 1964, Dr King received the **Nobel Peace Prize** for trying to change unfair **laws** peacefully. This is a picture of him receiving it.

Marches

This is a **memorial programme** from a **protest march** in Washington, D.C. in 1963. It shows when Dr King gave his "I Have a Dream" speech.

MARCH ON WASHINGTON FOR JOBS AND FREEDOM
AUGUST 28, 1963

LINCOLN MEMORIAL PROGRAM

1.	The National Anthem	*Led by* Marian Anderson.
2.	Invocation	The Very Rev. Patrick O'Boyle, *Archbishop of Washington.*
3.	Opening Remarks	A. Philip Randolph, *Director March on Washington for Jobs and Freedom.*
4.	Remarks	Dr. Eugene Carson Blake, *Stated Clerk, United Presbyterian Church of the U.S.A.; Vice Chairman, Commission on Race Relations of the National Council of Churches of Christ in America.*
5.	Tribute to Negro Women Fighters for Freedom Daisy Bates Diane Nash Bevel Mrs. Medgar Evers Mrs. Herbert Lee Rosa Parks Gloria Richardson	Mrs. Medgar Evers
6.	Remarks	John Lewis, *National Chairman, Student Nonviolent Coordinating Committee.*
7.	Remarks	Walter Reuther, *President, United Automobile, Aerospace and Agricultural Implement Wokers of America, AFL-CIO; Chairman, Industrial Union Department, AFL-CIO.*
8.	Remarks	James Farmer, *National Director, Congress of Racial Equality.*
9.	Selection	Eva Jessye *Choir*
10.	Prayer	Rabbi Uri Miller, *President Synagogue Council of America.*
11.	Remarks	Whitney M. Young, Jr., *Executive Director, National Urban League.*
12.	Remarks	Mathew Ahmann, *Executive Director, National Catholic Conference for Interracial Justice.*
13.	Remarks	Roy Wilkins, *Executive Secretary, National Association for the Advancement of Colored People.*
14.	Selection	Miss Mahalia Jackson
15.	Remarks	Rabbi Joachim Prinz, *President American Jewish Congress.*
16.	Remarks	The Rev. Dr. Martin Luther King, Jr., *President, Southern Christian Leadership Conference.*
17.	The Pledge	A Philip Randolph
18.	Benediction	Dr. Benjamin E. Mays, *President, Morehouse College.*

"WE SHALL OVERCOME"

Dr King wanted peaceful change but
sometimes things became violent. Here a
policeman lets his dog attack a black man
during a peaceful march.

Newspapers

This newspaper shows when the **Civil Rights Bill** was passed. These new **laws** ended many unfair rules. It was what Martin Luther King Jr. had worked for.

"All the News That's Fit to Print"

The New York Times.

LATE CITY EDITION
U. S. Weather Bureau Report (Page 50) Increases:
Fair and hot today and tomorrow.
Chance of late showers each day.
Temp. Range: 91—71; yesterday: 80—65
Temp.-Hum. Index: 80 to 85; yesterday: 74.

VOL. CXIII..No. 38,864.   © 1964 by The New York Times Company / Times Square, New York, N. Y. 10036   NEW YORK, SATURDAY, JUNE 20, 1964.   TEN CENTS

U.S. STRESSING IT WOULD FIGHT TO DEFEND ASIA

WARNING TO REDS

Commitment to Laos and South Vietnam Called Unlimited

By MAX FRANKEL
Special to The New York Times

WASHINGTON, June 19 —The Administration is saying more emphatically each day that North Vietnam and its closest ally, Communist China, must leave their neighbors alone or face a war with the United States.

In the minds of officials here the United States commitment to the security of Southeast Asia is now unlimited and comparable with the commitment to West Berlin.

In diplomatic terms this means the officials find themselves unable to negotiate with anything except the threat of force to persuade the Asian Communists to stop the efforts to "liberate" South Vietnam and Laos.

Thus far, the Administration is not sure that the Asian Communists have accurately interpreted the warning signals from Washington. It is not sure that its allies in Europe appreciate the gravity of the United States commitment. And it is not sure that the American people understand the reasons for it.

Decision Publicized

Accordingly, the word is being passed with increasing vigor to the Congress, to the Washington press corps and to the Western allies.

These official assertions suggest that the decision to deny Southeast Asia to Communism was, in effect, taken a long time ago through circumstance and a cumulative series of lesser decisions.

JOHNSON IS FIRM

Vows in California to Oppose Violators of Freedom in World

By TOM WICKER
Special to The New York Times

SAN FRANCISCO, June 19—President Johnson promised tonight to open an "offensive in the pursuit of peace" based on an overwhelming military power that "makes it possible to seek agreement without fearing loss of liberty."

The President, addressing an audience of nearly 2,500 at a Democratic party fund-raising dinner, also pledged stern American opposition to "those who believe they can violate their neighbor's borders and steal their neighbor's freedom."

At the end of a day in California during which he gave several indications that he expected to be President for at least four more years, Mr. Johnson said he wanted to double the size of the Peace Corps, pursue what he called the "great society" with "the vision and valor of pioneers" and achieve "full equality for all our people."

Earlier in the day, after an enthusiastic welcome from more than 360,000 San Franciscans who lined Market Street to see his motorcade, Mr. President came as near as he ever has to predicting his election in November.

Predicts the Good Life

"A Government which can get things done and knows where it is going," he said, is "the kind of Government you have had for the past four years and that is the kind of Government you are going to get for the next four years."

SENATOR KENNEDY HURT IN AIR CRASH; BAYH INJURED, TOO

Both Are in Fair Condition in Massachusetts Hospital —Pilot of Plane Killed

By The Associated Press

SOUTHAMPTON, Mass., Saturday, June 20—Senator Edward M. Kennedy, younger brother of President Kennedy, and Senator Birch Bayh were injured in the crash of a private plane last night while on the way to the Massachusetts Democratic Convention.

The pilot was killed and two other persons were injured. Mr. Kennedy was semiconscious.

Both Senators were reported in fair condition at Cooley Dickinson Hospital in nearby Northampton.

Also injured were Mrs. Bayh, reported in good condition, and Edward Moss of Andover, administrative aide to Mr. Kennedy, who was reported in critical condition.

The pilot was identified as Edwin J. Zimny, 48 years old, of Lawrence, a last-minute substitute for the regular Kennedy

Senator Edward M. Kennedy
Associated Press

CIVIL RIGHTS BILL PASSED, 73-27; JOHNSON URGES ALL TO COMPLY; DIRKSEN BERATES GOLDWATER

PRESIDENT'S PLEA

He Declares the Task Now Is to Change Law Into Custom

Special to The New York Times

SAN FRANCISCO, June 19—President Johnson called the Senate passage of his civil rights bill today a "challenge to men of good will in every part of the country to transform the commands of our law into the customs of our land."

Mr. Johnson said it was now the nation's task "to reach beyond the content of the bill to conquer the barriers of poor education, poverty, and squalid housing which are an inheritance of past injustice and an impediment to future advance."

He said that he did not "underestimate the depth of the passions involved in the struggle for racial equality."

But he also spoke of "a large reservoir of goodwill and compassion, of decency and fair play which seeks a vision of justice without violence in the streets."

Johnson Statement

If these forces, the President said, "do not desert the field, if they can be brought to the battle, then the years of trial will be a prelude to the final triumph of a land 'with liberty and justice for all.'"

The President issued his statement on the rights bill here, while he was beginning a two-day tour of California. The full text of the statement follows:

ON HAND FOR THE VOTE: Visitors waiting outside the Capitol yesterday before the vote on the civil rights bill was registered.
United Press International Telephoto

ACTION BY SENATE

Revised Measure Now Goes Back to House for Concurrence

By E. W. KENWORTHY
Special to The New York Times

WASHINGTON, June 19 — The Senate passed the civil rights bill today by a vote of 73 to 27.

The final roll-call came at 7:40 P.M. on the 83d day of debate, nine days after closure was invoked.

Voting for the bill were 46 Democrats and 27 Republicans. Voting against it were 21 Democrats and six Republicans.

Except for Senator Robert C. Byrd of West Virginia, all the Democratic votes against the bill came from Southerners.

Senator Barry Goldwater of Arizona voted against the bill, as he said yesterday he would. The five other Republicans opposing it all support Mr. Goldwater's candidacy for the Republican Presidential nomination.

They were Bourke B. Hickenlooper of Iowa, chairman of the Senate Republican Policy Committee; Norris Cotton of New Hampshire, Edwin L. Mechem of New Mexico, Milward L. Simpson of Wyoming and John G. Tower of Texas.

Pledge Acceptance

The bill will now go back to the House for concurrence in the changes that the Senate made in the measure the House passed last Feb. 10 by a vote of 290 to 130.

Tonight, Representative Emanuel Celler, Democrat of New York, and William M. McCulloch, Republican of Ohio,

---

ARIZONAN TARGET **Rights Bill Roll-Call Vote**
OF GOP LEADER

"Senate passage of the civil rights bill is a major step toward equal opportunities for all Americans. I congratulate Senators of both parties who

Gravesite

Every day hundreds of people visit Dr King's gravesite. The words cut into the stone say, "Free at Last, Free at Last. Thank God Almighty, I am Free at Last."

Glossary

This glossary explains difficult words, and helps you to say words which may be hard to say.

boycott stop going to a shop or using a service to **protest**

civil rights bill a **law** which makes sure people are treated fairly

courageous brave. You say *ka-rayjus*

doctorate degree the highest college degree a person can receive

equal rights everyone having the same rights, no matter what their race or religion is

laws rules

march a group of people walking together to show their support for something

memorial programme a list of what happens at a special event. You say *mim-awriul*

minister priest

mourned feel sad when someone dies

Nobel Peace Prize an award given each year to a person who works for peace

nonviolent not being violent or fighting back

protest to complain about an unfair **law**

seminary a college for people studying to become religious leaders. You say *semmin-ree*

Index